EAGLES' WINGS

An Uncommon Story of World War II

By Andrew Layton

Eagles' Wings
by Andrew Layton

Printed in the United States of America

ISBN 978-1-60266-390-9

www.xulonpress.com

Also by Andrew Layton

Wolverines in the Sky:
Michigan's Fighter Aces of WWI, WWII and Korea

*"You yourselves have seen what I did to Egypt,
and how I carried you on eagles' wings,
and brought you to myself"*
-Exodus 19:4

Acknowledgements

If there's one thing to learn about the publishing process, it's that writing a book is truly a team effort. Though only one person's name will eventually end up on the cover, the number of people who assist in making that cover a reality is almost unbelievable. Hopefully, I can hit the highlights in no specific order and give credit here to a few individuals who helped make this book possible. To these people, as well as those not listed, I sincerely give thanks. Each of them deserves far more recognition than this brief mention can provide.

- The **staff at the Battle Creek VA Medical Center**, especially **Margaret Trunick, Nancy Babcock, Todd Greenman, David Irvine** and **Patrick Gault;** for being a such great a encouragement over the years and for your role in initiating the Veteran's History Project in the Battle Creek area. Without you, the interviews that inspired this book would not have taken place.
- **Michael and Dorothy Martich**, for fueling my interest in history from the beginning and providing invaluable information on the Battle Creek Sanitarium and the impact of the Kellogg's Company on our community. Thanks also for opening the door to be a

part of the Battle Creek Federal Center's Centennial Celebration Committee through which I originally met Mr. Jenkins.

- **Our South Side Bible Church Family Members** for their unlimited encouragement and advice.
- To Secretary of Veterans Affairs **Jim Nicholson**, former VA Under Secretary of Health **Jonathan Perlin** and Director of VA Voluntary Service **Laura Balun** for their encouragement and generosity in opening many doors for the future.
- My parents, **Joe and Amy Layton,** for all they have done for me over the years, which includes taking on the role of home educators.
- Proofreaders **Shelly Smyth**, **Larry Gordon** and **Brett Tuttle.** Your assistance is greatly appreciated.
- Former Senator **Bob Dole** and Senator **Daniel K. Inouye** for their gracious comments.
- Of course, **Larry Jenkins** and **Jack Curtis** themselves, who first of all lived the contents of this book. It has been a true honor to work with them on this project, and though it has been a long process, the efforts of writing pale dramatically compared to what they have endured for our country.
- And finally, my Lord and Savior **Jesus Christ**, who has offered me far more opportunities in life than I deserve.

Thanks again to these, and all the others who played a role in the production of this book. Your assistance is appreciated more than you know.

Contents

Author's Note

By definition, a hero is someone noted for his feats of courage or nobility who has risked or sacrificed his life on someone else's behalf. This book is about two men who are indeed heroes: Jack Curtis and Larry Jenkins. Their uncommon story has been an inspiration to me since the day I met them, and now it has been my privilege to aid in the process of bringing that story to you in the form of this book.

A bulk of the text is derived from two interviews that were conducted while I was a fourteen-year-old freshman in high school. Neither was performed with any inclination that they would one day find themselves inspiring a publication of any kind. However, as the idea of this work progressed, I found that the original interviews would in fact provide a very effective way to present the incredible stories that were captured in the veteran's original words. Hopefully, these words will still hold the same power on paper as they did when they were first spoken into the tape recorder.

While initially preparing this manuscript, I struggled to come up with a title for the project that would be both appropriate and meaningful. It wasn't until I was thumbing through my Bible one evening that a phrase from Exodus 19:4 came to my attention and consequently rooted itself into my mind.

"You yourselves have seen what I did to Egypt, and how I carried you on eagles' wings, and brought you to myself."

As I thought about this passage, I realized that it would indeed serve as an appropriate heading for more reasons then one. God was speaking these words to the Israelites just three months after they had been freed from bondage under the hand of Pharaoh. He had delivered them from the terror of captivity through means unexplainable to the faithless, which are represented figuratively by the concept of "eagles' wings." Through these supernatural methods, God had revealed himself to the Israelites as One deserving of complete worship and faith.

The parallels between this account and the story that Jack Curtis and Larry Jenkins tell were impossible to ignore. Like the Israelites, both endured a brutal period of suffering and captivity but somehow survived due to events they themselves often do not understand to this day. Both men cite their near-death experiences as having strengthened their faith in God and both have confided that had His hand not been upon them, neither would have lived to relate their experiences in the first place. It was as if they too had been carried on Eagles' Wings like the Israelites of old.

Though this book is not a memoir, the events chronicled here are entirely true and are recorded almost exactly as they were recalled in those initial interviews. My goal is that through these examples, you will ultimately come to a deeper appreciation of what that word *hero* really means.

Andrew Layton
Battle Creek, Michigan
March, 2007

Eagle's Wings

Introduction

"What are the Chances?"

I magine for a moment that you are a twenty-two year old First Lieutenant in the United States Army Air Corps. The date is May 16, 1945, and you are being processed in at a U.S. Army medical facility in Reims, France. Just four days ago, you were freed from a Nazi prison camp by an American tank division after more than eight months of dismal captivity. Although your heart leapt at the idea of simply being free, you couldn't run to meet your liberators because of the full body cast that encased your left side. Beneath that cast were the scars on your leg where shrapnel had ripped most of the flesh away when your plane was shot down behind enemy lines.

For Jack Curtis, all of the above was true.

Like many other American servicemen who saw combat during World War II, overseas duty had not been pleasant for Curtis. As a seasoned navigator on B-24 heavy bombers, he had been shot down and captured on his thirty-first mission over Southern Europe. His left leg had indeed been shattered by shrapnel, and his harrowing parachute jump only served to compound his wounds. Just after landing, Curtis had been arrested by a German infantry detachment and was locked away for more than eight months of captivity in an Austrian prison camp. Most of it he experienced from the vantage point of that excruciating full body cast. But now, after his liberation, Jack was finally headed home. This small French hospital was one of the last stops in a series of required medical and administrative processes before his final shipment back to the United States. The end of his nightmare was finally in sight.

As he and many of the other newly-freed men settled into their quarters that afternoon, Curtis saw another Air Force Lieutenant - his legs bandaged with plaster casts - crutch down the hallway to the window at the end of the room. The man, who could have passed for a high school freshman, looked vaguely familiar, but Jack wasn't able to put a name with the man's face.

Later that evening, Curtis had difficulty getting to sleep. Perhaps it was the memories of stress and fear from the POW camp that just kept coming back to him. He lit a cigarette, hoping it would help him relax. The guy in the next bed over, who was called Smitty, was restless too. So he joined Curtis for a smoke, and they got to talking.

"Where're you from?" Smitty asked.

Jack paused for a second, perhaps reflecting back on more peaceful memories of home. "Battle Creek, Michigan."

"No Kidding?" answered Smitty, surprised by Jack's response. "I think we've got another guy in here from Battle Creek, too."

Jack too was surprised; "Was it that guy who came through here earlier today on crutches?

"Yeah, it was. Do you know him?"

Jack suddenly realized who the man was that he had been watching a few hours before. It was his childhood friend and schoolmate Larry Jenkins, whom he had not heard from since they went into the service some three years prior. Larry's already thin frame must have dwindled to even less during his imprisonment, which explained to Jack why he didn't recognize him at first.

"Sure I know him; went to high school and played baseball with him when I was a kid."

Smitty laughed. "Well I'll be darned - what are the chances?"

The next morning, Larry Jenkins woke up early and took a walk around the hospital on his crutches. He had also been through a lot in the past two years or so, and he was thankful just to be alive right now – and free. Like Jack, Larry had been shot down and captured over occupied Europe, and had suffered horrendous injuries to both legs, narrowly escaping death on several occasions. The funny thing was, he was barely twenty years old and looked about fifteen. Because of this, his friends had dubbed this battered combat veteran "Junior".

As Larry continued with his walk that morning, he made his way down the hallway past Jack Curtis's bed again, looking for Smitty. Jack, who was still immobile in a full body cast, spoke to him.

"Hey Larry, remember me?"

Without even turning to see who it was, Jenkins recognized the voice and laughed. "By golly… how are you doing, Jack Curtis? …What are the chances of seeing you here?"

"What are the chances?"

This phrase is hardly sufficient to describe the situation.

We now jump ahead to December 3, 2002 - the day I first met Larry Jenkins. I had volunteered to participate in a local research project to record oral histories from several World War II era veterans who received care at the Percy Jones Army Hospital which was located in our hometown of Battle Creek, Michigan. In addition to local archiving, we decided that the tapes would also be sent to the Library of Congress where they would be safeguarded under the Veterans History Project, a national initiative to preserve the tales of service from our nation's veterans. Because these interviews were being conducted in anticipation of the sixtieth anniversary of the hospital's opening, My dad, Joe, and I asked Larry and his wife Peg to come to the old hospital building, which now houses the Hart-Dole-Inuoye Federal Center, to share some of their memories that took place in that very same facility so many years before.

As we greeted Mr. and Mrs. Jenkins outside the building, I could sense a deep emotion in Larry's voice that made it clear how excited he was to visit the old hospital again. I had been to my dad's workplace at the Federal Center countless times before, but having Larry there made it a whole new experience. Entering the lobby that day was like stepping into a time machine. Within moments of our arrival, Mr. Jenkins had transported us back to a summer day in 1945 when he was carried through that very same doorway for the first time on a stretcher - a twenty year-old disabled veteran with his legs encased in a plaster cast. As I listened to him talk, I found myself mesmerized. It was probably five or ten minutes before I remembered why we were here – to give the Jenkins's a tour of the building and to record some of their recollections on tape. "Where would you like to go for the interview?" I asked. It took about a quarter of a second for Larry to reply. "The 10th floor – that's where my bed was you know." "Then you lead the way, Mr. Jenkins." And with that we headed off to the elevator which took us to up to Larry's old floor - the officer's ward.

As we got off the elevator, Larry was amazed at how much the rooms, now converted to office space, had changed. "I barely recognize the place," he said as we walked through the hallway. He pointed a few things out to us, but seemed a little disappointed that it was so different than he remembered. Then his eyes lit up. "Wait a minute. I think this is it!" We followed him through a doorway right into someone's office but had no idea what he was talking about. Finally, he stopped at a large window, obviously overwhelmed with emotion. "Yes. I'm sure of it. This is exactly where my bed was. I laid here and looked out this window every day for more than two years, wondering if I would ever walk again." By now, I could see the tears streaming down his face, and for a few moments, I couldn't help but feel some of the emotion too. We were quiet for a long time. "This brings back so many memories," Larry said, breaking the silence. "So many memories... some bad and some good ... but mostly good".

We stayed there in Larry's old ward room for a few more minutes before continuing on with our tour which turned out to be one of the most informative three-hour periods I have ever experienced. Not surprisingly, Larry ended up guiding a lot more of it than my dad did. His memories of the building interestingly seemed to focus not on his own experiences there, but about the friends he made while a patient who influenced him in his recovery. One of the friends he mentioned was Jack Curtis, also from Battle Creek. We had gone to church with Mr. Curtis for several years and knew him pretty well, but had no idea that he too was a decorated World War II veteran who spent time in recovery at Percy Jones. As Larry told us about the remarkable friendship he and Jack had formed during their stay at the hospital, I knew that Mr. Curtis would also have an amazing story to tell, and I was interested to hear his perspective of what life was like at the hospital, too. Several months later, I had the privilege of conducting a similar interview with Mr. Curtis at the Battle Creek VA Medical Center, but we will get to that story later.

After spending time with both men and listening to them talk in detail about their experiences, I was absolutely amazed by the incredible lives both have led. But most impressive to me was the way they considered their military service to be anything but unique. In their minds, they were ordinary guys who were "just doing their jobs" – like the fifteen million others who served in uniform during the Second World War.

Even now as I read through these interviews, I find myself asking the question, "What are the chances?" Two men who had grown up just blocks away from each other, who shared so much in common during their wartime service without even realizing it, meeting once again in a French hospital for ex-POW's. *"What are the chances?"* is right.

Hollywood couldn't have come up with a better story.

Part One:

Jack Curtis

Chapter 1

"Magic"

In the mid 1930's, Battle Creek, Michigan was still very much a small town. With a population of about 40,000, it was in many ways similar to any other rural Midwestern community of that period. Battle Creek looked like your average all-American town from a distance. It was filled with churches, homes, and a few small shops and factories here and there. But Battle Creek was also set distinctly apart by a title that no other town in the world could claim – "The Cereal City".

Battle Creek's longtime association with the breakfast cereal companies began in 1875, when a young doctor named John Harvey Kellogg made his presence known in the community after his appointment as director of the Western Health Reform Institute. Thanks to the charisma and medical genius of Dr. Kellogg, the Institute grew from a small Seventh-Day Adventist hospital to a nationally esteemed medical facility. In 1895, Kellogg's legacy was solidified when he sparked America's first health food craze by crafting a new product that would change the way breakfast was to be eaten forever. This creation, which Kellogg referred to as "corn flakes", instantly ushered as many as eighty imitation companies into the Battle Creek area who hoped to cash in on some of Kellogg's success. As a result of this industrial boom, Battle Creek - the cereal bowl of America - was brought to national prominence in a way that had never been seen before.

Perhaps nothing embodied the glory of those days more effectively than the Battle Creek Sanitarium. Built by Dr. Kellogg in 1903, the "San" as it was affectionately known, was a magical place; a palace-like resort designed to promote a healthy lifestyle among the rich and famous by showcasing Kellogg's many edible innovations. With its massive twin towers looming at the impressive height of 14 stories and its gigantic facade spanning the east side of the building, the Sanitarium looked like something out of a dream. And that was only the exterior. Once you got through the doors, the San was a haven of unbelievable luxury that rivaled any mansion in the country; or the world for that matter. Thanks to this extraordinary atmosphere, celebrities and millionaires such as Henry Ford, Theodore Roosevelt, John Rockefeller, and Thomas Edison flocked to rural Battle Creek in hopes of learning a better way of life from Dr. Kellogg and his world-class staff. But by the early 1930's, the golden age of Battle Creek had faded. Though the Sanitarium still highlighted the city's skyline, its struggles to stay in business had become well-publicized due to a seventy-five percent drop in patients since the stock market crash of 1929. Financial issues also plagued Battle Creek's cereal companies during the depression, and by 1930, only two competitors to the Kellogg's Company remained in operation; Post and General Mills.

Though the San's golden age had clearly faded by the early 1930's, it at least still captured the imagination of an eight-year-old Jack Curtis. While making his way home from school on any given day, Jack was likely to cut across the Sanitarium's lawn as he headed to his house located just up the hill on Walters Street. But Jack's eye would often turn to the inviting courtyards and fancy cars parked along the San's sprawling circle driveway. Perhaps he would stop on the grass for a few moments to read off the names of each state represented there by a license plate. "*Maine...Georgia...California...Missouri...*"

Usually, a voice would interrupt Jack about now, and a conversation not unlike this one would probably follow:

"Get off this lawn, kid... I thought I told you never to come onto Sanitarium property again!" Jack would look up at an angry security guard. "But sir, I live in this neighborhood and I was just looking at those cars..." The guard would cut him off. "What's your name son?"

"Jack Curtis"

"Well, son, I don't care where you live or how much you like looking at cars. I'm sorry, but *nobody* trespasses on the San's lawn, and that's final. Now you run on home and don't ever let me see you around here again." "Yes sir" the boy would reply, hanging his head.

The guard couldn't blame Jack for his curiosity in the building. You see, in 1932, nothing in the entire city of Battle Creek could match the splendor and luxury of the Sanitarium. Not only did the circle driveway serve as a perfect place to spot fancy cars with out-of-state licenses, but sometimes you could even catch a glimpse of someone famous who had come to enjoy the beautiful facility and its friendly staff. But even more exciting than this was that feeling you got when you looked up at the San's two massive towers looming in the sky, dripping with enough ambiance to set your imagination running. To eight-year-old Jack Curtis, the Battle Creek Sanitarium was more than just an expensive resort. To him it was magic. And how lucky he considered himself to have such magic in what was practically his own back yard.

Chapter 2

"A Whirlwind Journey"

We now fast forward through time some seventy-one years to June 5, 2003. I was waiting in the lobby of the Battle Creek VA Medical Center for Mr. Curtis to arrive, anxiously awaiting our interview that was to take place in just a few moments. As I saw his car enter the parking lot, I headed out the door and into the light drizzle to meet him. His "Ex-POW" license plate caught my eye as we exchanged greetings and proceeded back into the building, through the covered tunnels that connect each facility on the VA's campus. Though he walked with a cane, I noticed that Mr. Curtis's robust frame projected a warm impression of vigor that made him seem younger than his seventy-nine years. After several minutes, we finally arrived at building thirteen, which housed the VA's television studio; the predetermined site of our discussion. As Mr. Curtis and I engaged in small talk, we made ourselves comfortable in preparation for the interview. I wondered then if Mr. Curtis was as excited about this as I was.

When the media technicians had finished preparing the equipment, the "roll tape" signal was given, and I embarked with Mr. Curtis on a whirlwind journey into the past - his past - that soon had me lost in his words and the images they stirred up in my mind. Besides an occasional nod or a brief question, I just sat back and took in the experience as he told his story.

"I was born on July 26, 1923 in Charlotte, Michigan," he began, "but I've lived my whole life in Battle Creek..."

...My dad was a barber, which meant that during the great depression times were very hard for us. People would rather go without a haircut or cut their own hair than pay for the luxury of a barber. So we moved around a lot and tried to make it the best we could. One of the places we lived was on Walters Avenue, which was important because it was near the Kellogg's Sanitarium in a largely Seventh-Day Adventist neighborhood. A lot of my friends went to the Seventh-Day church and we wouldn't see them from Friday night all the way through Saturday because that was their Sabbath. But anyway, I ended up graduating from Lakeview High School in 1941. I was working nights for the Kellogg Company and was commuting to Western Michigan University in Kalamazoo during the day, but with the "Yellow Peril", as the Japanese were called then, threatening to seize control of the Western Pacific and the German *Wehrmacht* raising hell in the North Atlantic, like millions of other young men my age, I couldn't wait to get into the fight. The Army Air Corps was promising cadets a chance to fly and defend American freedom, and it was a chance I couldn't pass up. So I enlisted in the Army Air Corps in December of 1942. The most amazing thing was that after I enlisted, I took all the tests to get into the aviation cadets, but got a little white card that said, "You're deferred until June 1946." Well, that obviously didn't happen, and I was called to active duty in February of 1943.

I went to basic training in Fresno, California. Incidentally, we were at the fairgrounds there and the previous occupants of the facility were the Japanese who were being interned by our government, which was a tragic activity. From Fresno, I went to Santa Ana for classification, and I was fortunate enough to qualify for all three programs: the pilot, navigation, and bombardier schools. I soloed after about five hours at Visalia Primary Flight School in California, but they didn't like the way I landed airplanes. So after more than a hundred landings, the instructor said, "Jack, maybe you would be better off doing something else." So I selected navigation training which I got at Hondo, Texas.

After completing that, I was commissioned as a Second Lieutenant and got a few days off to come home. I then went through a series of stops, starting in Lincoln Nebraska, and finally ending in Boise, Idaho, where I was in the training program with my crew. We pulled our crew together there, and from there went back to Lincoln, Nebraska, and then on to our port of embarkation, which was Hampton Rhodes, Virginia. Officially, I was to serve my time in combat with the 514th Bomb Squadron, a subdivision of the 376th Bomb Group, which was part of the 15th Air Force. As a unit, we took a ship overseas to Naples, Italy. We spent a few days there and finally I wound up in the town of San Pancrazio in Southern Italy. It was a dirty little community that was largely supported by the wine industry. You'd see people walking around with stains on their feet from the wine presses because that was how a majority of them made their living. It was very dirty though, and very poor. It was really too bad to see. But that base in San Pancrazio was the base that I flew thirty-one combat missions from. Well, I completed thirty, and I didn't come home from my thirty-first. So Andy, I think that gives you a quick review up to the time I was shot down.

By now, I was totally enthralled, and I was dying to hear more from Mr. Curtis.

"Can you describe some of the details of that last mission for us?"

Yes, I can, Andy. Some of them are still pretty vivid in my mind. We were assigned to bomb a railroad bridge at Marburg, Yugoslavia. At that time in the war, Germany was pulling its troops and its armaments out of Greece, Bulgaria, and the Balkans. Of course bombing the bridge would be an impediment to getting their equipment and their manpower back. We came into the target area I think around twenty-four thousand feet. I can't remember just exactly, but I do remember that the target was obscured by clouds. So we circled the area for almost an hour, gradually letting down to 18,000 feet, which gave the German radar ample opportunity to get a lock on us. By the time we came back over the target, they had pretty well zeroed in with their anti-aircraft guns. Just after the bombardier called "bombs away", our aircraft took a mortal hit from the flack bursts.

Chapter 3

"The First Scary Thing"

The explosion blew a huge hole in the right side of the airplane and damaged two of our engines. Pieces of those anti-aircraft shell fragments tore away much of the flesh and muscle around my left knee. I forced myself to a kneeling position and manually cranked open the nose turret door so that the nose gunner and bombardier could get out. I showed the gunner where his parachute was – he always put it in the same place anyway – and then I bailed out. By then, both port engines were aflame and the plane was banking steeply to the left. Of our 11-man crew, we lost seven that day, either in the plane, or if some of them did make it out, we never heard what happened to them. Whether their chutes didn't open or whether they were killed once they got to the ground, we don't know. To this day I find it hard to believe that only four comrades survived that mission. Anyway, I pulled my ripcord relatively soon after getting out of the plane and I had a long float down… in silence.

I nodded, riveted to Mr. Curtis's words.

It was perfect silence…until they started shooting at me…There was no sensation of movement, I guess because there was no point of reference. But they shot at me as I was coming down, and I could hear bullets whizzing all around me. Fortunately, I wasn't hit, so far as I know.

When I hit the ground, I smashed my leg up really good. My leg had already been torn up pretty bad by the shrapnel and the landing shattered my left femur which left the jagged end of the broken bone jutting out through my thigh. My parachute had formed kind of a canopy over me, and when I pawed that off, I found myself looking up the barrels of a number of German rifles. But they didn't shoot me. When they saw the painful extent of my helplessness, two of them knelt down and tried to straighten out my smashed leg. They fashioned a crude splint to keep the broken bone in place and put a tourniquet just above my knee to staunch the flow of blood.

A couple of civilians had made their way to the scene as well, and one of them gave me an apple. I had lost a lot of blood, so I asked for some water, and they gave that to me, too. I was just absolutely dumbfounded that the very same people who had tried to kill me, and that I had been trying to kill just minutes earlier, were now trying to save my life. This is a difficult thing for me to explain exactly, but if there is a better commercial against war, I can't think of one. It was just that remarkable.

I nodded again to indicate my agreement.

They put me on a two-wheeled cart pulled by a horse, and took me to what I considered to be some kind of a first aid station. Then the first scary thing happened. They pulled back my flight suit and gave me a shot right in my breast. Of course, I had no idea whether this was going to kill me or what. I subsequently found out it was a tetanus shot.

There were some other non-Germans around this aid station, and I figured out that they were people who had been taken prisoner earlier. I think they were British, for the most part. They gave me a few cigarettes, which I used in those days, so I was happy to have them. The cigarettes didn't last long though because the Germans confiscated them. Then they took me to a small hospital, where I stayed for four days, still in my bloody rags. I had spoken with no one who knew English since those fellows gave me the cigarettes. But finally, they (the Germans) put me in a body cast, propped me up on a wooden seat and sent me by train to Graz, Austria. That's where I would spend my longest period of time as a prisoner.

Chapter 4

"Gratz"

The hospital in Gratz was, as far as I know, an orthopedic hospital. We had heard that they had a thousand patients there (mostly German) to take care of. There were only three surgeons to look after a caseload like that. They took me up to a ward room on the top floor. There I met the people who were going to be my room mates. I got shot down on October 14, so it was probably around the nineteenth when I arrived at this hospital. In that room, there were several other Americans, and also Italians, French, Russians, Australians, New Zealanders, a South African and even a Tasmanian. So we had a regular mixture of nationalities.

The room was about seventy feet long and they had beds going down both sides. They had spaced them just far enough apart that you could stretch your arm out and pass things around from bed to bed. The room was unheated for the most part, and it did little good to even try to heat it because most of the windows had been blown out by bomb blasts. There was just one little stove covered with ceramic tile in the corner, but it was only big enough to accommodate a small fire. You could have lit a box of matches and done about as much good. On top of that, the bedding they provided us was little more than a sheet, so we were always cold. The food was what you might expect; not too much, not too appetizing. But it did keep me alive, though I lost a lot of weight.

The real problem at Graz was my leg. It got infected quite badly. So they operated on me a couple of times, put me in traction for a short period of time, and then back into a cast. As a matter of fact, the only time I was ever warm was while I was in traction, because they put sort of a tent around my leg with a little light bulb in there, and that did give off some heat.

The strange thing was that all of the beds on the outer wall had mirrors attached to them, and they gave us those so that we could watch the planes come overhead without straining our necks whenever there was a raid. So when the sirens started going off, we'd get the bombers in our mirrors and watch them come across in their formations. As they got closer, you'd begin to hear what sounded like freight trains coming down from the sky, and those were the bombs falling. It was a sound that you could feel deep within your stomach, and it was terrible. Then the anti-aircraft guns on the ground would open up, and it got even louder. I'm not sure if it was a violation of the Geneva convention or not, but the Germans seemed to have all the big guns concentrated around the hospital, because they figured they were less likely to get hit there. Either way, it was a dirty trick. So the American bombers would come during the day, and then at night the British Lancasters would come in for their runs. We could only see these little flickers of light in our mirrors from their engines at first, but then as they got closer, they would send out these gigantic flares that lit up the sky like day so they could see their targets. It was always a mixed emotion when these raids would come because you knew they were your friends who were going after your captors, but at the same time it was really quite terrifying.

Later on, when they'd have a bombing raid, they would evacuate us to a sub basement of the hospital, beds and all. But finally, because it took so much effort moving me around, they just left me down there with two other POW's. I recall one little tiny light bulb in that room. We saw people from the outside world only when they brought us food and on those rare occasions when we saw a doctor. We did have a wind-up Victrola put near enough my bed so I could operate it. We had three records that we listened to constantly. My favorite was of Dinah Shore singing "Memphis Blues." Would you believe I think I can still sing that song without missing a word?

Surprisingly, we were permitted to write home on occasion, though it was rather infrequent. Some of those letters actually did get through to my family. I think I got about three letters from them in the eight months I was in captivity. But by that time, the Germans didn't have very much, and I'm sure that getting a prisoner's mail out came pretty low on their list of priorities.

Chapter 5

"Liberated"

It must have been February or March when they moved me from Graz to another location – Lienz it think it was called. It was a little nicer, a little more modern, but the treatment and food were about the same. We weren't there for very long. I can't tell you for sure how long it was, but we knew then there was reason to believe that the war was winding down. You could tell that because we began to get friendlier treatment. I had never really been abused all along, but what I mean is all of a sudden they started saying things like, "Hey Joe, you know my brother? He lives in Chicago." We knew they were trying to butter us up a little.

Eventually, they put us on a hospital train, and we were on that for about four or five days. I wound up being moved to a spa in Germany called Bad Gestein. It was the same spa that the Roosevelt's had used prewar. The treatment and food there was much better. Finally, sometime in the neighborhood of twelve days after the war was over in Europe, we were liberated by an American tank outfit.

So from Bad Gestein we went to, let's see... Munich. Next it was a field hospital and then to Reims, France, then to Paris, then Presque Isle, Maine, and then to Percy Jones Army Hospital, ironically in my hometown of Battle Creek.

Now, I'll tell you just a couple of interesting things about that. Perhaps the most memorable for me came one day when we were scheduled to be flown back to the states and I happened to get on an ambulance with another serviceman who had been burned very badly. Whenever the ambulance hit a bump, he would groan, and he must have been suffering horribly. So we went at a very slow pace. By the time we got to...I think it was Orley Field in Paris...the plane was gone. So they took us back to the same ward we had come from in Reims. Well, that evening, the ward filled up with new people who were on their way back to the United States, as I was.

In the middle of the night, I wasn't sleeping too well. Someone a couple beds down lit a cigarette. I guess I lit a cigarette too, and we got to talking. He said "Where are you from", and I said "Battle Creek." He said, "Battle Creek, we've got a man in our group from there, too." And I said, "Well, was it that man that came through this afternoon on crutches that went down to the end of the room and then left?" He said, "Yes, it was...do you know him?" And I said, "Yeah, I do, I went to high school with him."

And that of course was Larry Jenkins.

Larry and I were processed together in Reims and shared a hospital room in Paris. He was ambulatory on crutches and I wasn't. When we came back to the States, we both wound up at Percy Jones, and we are still very close friends to this day. Very close. We fished together in Canada every spring for about forty years, and he is absolutely the best guide and motor boat driver on earth. I've always said if I was going to be marooned on a desert island, he's the guy I'd want to have with me. He's a very capable individual.

Chapter 6

"A Hospital or a Hotel?"

So now, I've got you back to Percy Jones. The hospital building was that old place built by the Kellogg's to use as their Sanitarium. It had been purchased by the Army and converted in 1943. Little did I realize that my youthful playground would now become my hospital. I doubt that there was another place on earth that would fit our needs so well. There were those severely injured and barely alive, and those who were recovering quite well. Among them were quadruple amputees (amps), triple amps, double amps, and hundreds of amputees with parts of arms and legs missing or severely damaged. Because of the extraordinary care we received, many patients came to the conclusion that this was no hospital, but a hotel. Not all of us uttered these words, but many of my close Percy Jones buddies did. The phrase was often used when one of our bedmates started complaining, usually over a trivial matter. And then, when a patient went too far with the likes of a wait-on-me-now attitude, we reversed the slogan and reminded him that this is not a hotel, this is a hospital. While Percy Jones was thought of primarily as an orthopedic and amputee's hospital, there were also many plastic surgery patients, those with neurological problems, and those with memory loss and other types of injuries.

Larry and I were processed in at Percy Jones by a doctor that everyone loved so much – Dr. Gilfallen. By that time, my leg had gotten bad. The fracture of the femur had knit and so it was decided that there wasn't really anything more that could be done. I'd lost about three and a half inches in the length of my left leg and my left knee was stiff. It had fused in the cast over that interim period after I was shot down.

As a group, we were winding down from the unknown where we knew not what the day would hold for us, such as being POW's, or daily front line combat for some of the others. The evidence of our experience was not just the scars or missing body parts, but the infamous battle dreams for those who continued to fight the war every night. Often, the rooms were filled with cries, moans, profanity, and shouts.

The physical arrangements of the hospital were typically ward rooms, with as many as twelve beds. Whether it was a planned matter or simply a building configuration, the grouping of fellow patients was fortunate. The camaraderie played right into our hands, as the bedmate interactions became a big part of the healing process. Those who did not join the often-irreverent interplay and exchanges (like those who just plain gave up) often did not progress towards healing like the others. Many had a very severe injury and yet could tolerate such ribbing as, "Look, you've got a million-dollar wound there, Stubby" or "I see you've got a pretty bad hangnail." Those who tried to buck the patient-imposed system either conformed or found themselves as minor outcasts going against an irreversible system.

The food at Percy Jones was good too, and so much better than what we had been used to. As one who lost seventy pounds in the POW camps, I would get a bottle of milk and a jar of mayonnaise on my tray every day. Milkshakes came in the afternoon, and later a beer or so would aid in the fattening process. Many top entertainers played at Percy Jones, too, such as Bob Hope, Bing Crosby and Stan Kenton. When I heard Dinah Shore was coming, I told a guy in Special Services about how we used to sit in that sub-basement room in Austria, listening to the wind up record of her singing "Memphis Blues" hundreds of times over. When Dinah finally made her visit, they must have told her, because she came into my room and sat on my bed. I told her the story, and of course she held my hand and sang "Memphis Blues" to me.

The staff at Percy Jones was super. Many of the nurses wound up as wife to one of their ward patients, and the doctors were all greatly respected as well. They were fondly referred to as "doc" by all. Dr. Gilfallen, as I mentioned earlier, was truly loved, and his miracle amputee work endeared him to many. The top orthopedic doctor, by the name of McKeever, had the same great respect. One very funny incident involved a patient with severe bone, muscle and nerve injuries to his lower arm and hand. When he returned from convalescent leave, his identical twin brother came along. We prevailed upon him to don hospital pajamas and get into his patient brother's bed for ward rounds. The double take on the doctor's face when he viewed what appeared to be a miracle recovery was an unforgettable sight. Fortunately, the doctor took it in the proper spirit.

I was also fortunate enough to meet and get to know quite well Daniel (Danny) Inouye, who has of course been the United States Senator from Hawaii for more than forty years now. But to us, he was always "Ding Ho." Danny was one of the most popular patients. He and I were good friends, and we partied together a lot. That seemed to be a pretty important part of our lives in those days. After being shot at, or as in my case, incarcerated as a POW, there were a lot of things we wanted to catch up on, and I am not sure I would have conducted myself exactly like that had I have gone through it later on.

But Danny and I became real good friends. I hadn't been paid in a year-and-a-half I guess, and we had priority to purchase a car. So I bought a brand new Oldsmobile, and Danny wanted to learn how to drive it. Danny was just fascinated with the thought of driving that car. So, I got a little spinner fastened on the steering wheel for him and because he had lost his right arm overseas, I taught him how to drive with one arm. He drove my car around and around the hospital compound and loved every minute of it. He and I have talked about that several times since.

I also got to know future Senator and Presidential Candidate Bob Dole at the hospital, though I was on ward ten and he was on ward nine. I used to visit down there every once and a while, and I recall playing bridge with him on occasion. He, Danny and Phil Hart, who was another Senator-to-be, were all in the same ward room at one time, and that's a remarkable coincidence. You can read that story in Tom Brokaw's book. Today they have even renamed the building the Hart-Dole-Inouye Federal Center in their honor.

I've stayed in touch with both Bob and Danny over the years, and I guess we've have had occasion to meet three or four times each. I've been to Washington and had lunch in the Senate dining room with Danny and I have run into him on a couple of occasions as well. My wife and I were at an airport one time, in line to get a seat assignment to Hawaii, and Danny was in the same line. Later on, I was in California on company business checking into the Oakland Hilton, and Danny and I were in the same line again. Most recently, when I remarried, my wife Phyllis and I took a delayed honeymoon to Hawaii and Maui. We decided not to have breakfast at the resort one morning and went into town instead. As we were going back, we passed a beautiful Methodist Church and I said, "Phyllis, let's go to church there this morning." So, we did. The church was open on both sides, and it was really a beautiful building. Some of the singing was even in the native tongue. But anyway, I'm sitting there, and Phyllis said to me, "Jack isn't that your friend Danny over there?" I said, "Oh Phyllis, I don't think so", but I looked over and incredible as it seems, for the third time, there he was! I went over, tapped him on the shoulder, and he said "Jack Curtis, what are you doing here?" It really was quite a coincidence. We chatted for quite a while. His parting words to me were, "Well, Jack, where will it be next time, Timbuktu?" That was the last time I have spoken directly with him to date, though we have exchanged letters with some regularity since then.

It's funny how the fact that I happened to know a couple of well-known celebrities and senators way back when has almost made me sort of a local icon, I guess. You'd be surprised how many people come up to me and say "Hey Jack, how's your old buddy Bob Dole doing?" They say it just as if I'd spent a lot of time with him the day before, or something.

But there were many other good friends that I made at Percy Jones, too. One man, Si Johnson, had been a track and field star in college and wound up playing a very credible game of golf on crutches, despite his amputation above the knee. He was also the one who wrote the words to that infamous hospital anthem. The opening line was "Percy Jones, Percy Jones, where they cut off all your bones!"

Herbie was another great guy in our bunch who was a double leg amp. He loved to go downtown to the Sky Club where he would regularly have to teach his date how to dance with him, wheelchair and all! Then there was Shadrack O'Saughnessy, the resident entertainer. His pay never lasted until the next payday. We couldn't bear not having him in the group, so we would regularly pay his way for him. Whenever we would go to the hospital annex on Dickman Road, Shadrack knew that the guards would have to check the trunk of the car at the gate before they let us in. Shad insisted one time that we put him in there, which we did. Needless to say, he startled the guard - big time - when the trunk was opened. This merely added to our reputation as being a group to watch out for.

The Annex... now that was where all the fun was. It was a complex of about fifteen or twenty buildings at Fort Custer that had been converted to house patients from Percy Jones. They would rotate around for periods of recuperation. Each building could hold about twenty-five guys, but they were all connected by a long hall. At the end of the hallway was a club where most of the less ambulatory patients spent a lot of time. They sold beer there, but you had to bring your own bottle. There was also a kitchen in each one, as well as a latrine and of course the large ward room. This was the healing arena. Privacy, forget it, and again the closeness, camaraderie and informal needling system did its fine work.

The real plus of the Annex, however, was Eagle Lake, with its snack bar and great swimming beach. I recall that when VJ day occurred, a big party was planned. I was still in a body cast from chest to hip on one side, and the other leg fully in the cast. I told the doctor to get me a gurney because I had to go to that party. He approved and I went. Well, it was worth it because one pretty nurse came up to me that night, put her arms around me, and gave me a great big kiss that made me shiver right down to my toes.

I finally got out of that cast in October. I had been in that thing or a similar one since I had been a prisoner. So after we became ambulatory, we spent a lot of time on convalescent leave, usually two months at a time. Since Battle Creek was my hometown, I used the annex as my hotel and would spend several days with my non-ambulatory buddies. When not on leave, one doctor would give us passes whenever we wanted. He could only authorize three days, but often he would give us a signed pass but without dates. If we were in a tough spot, we just filled in the dates. Unfortunately, that doctor was "retired" during his stint at the Annex. I suppose we aided in that happening.

There were a lot of others besides the three Senators –and it's very important to recognize that – who went on to very successful careers in all kinds of fields. For instance, double leg amputee John Swainson went on to become the State Supreme

Court Justice and later Governor of Michigan. Harold Russell, who lost both of his arms in combat, later won an Oscar for his movie role in *The Best Years of Our Lives*.

Percy Jones was just perfect for the patients. The staff and doctors were very solicitous about our care. I really can't say enough about the treatment I received at Percy Jones. I was there for a total of about two years, receiving various kinds of rehabilitation, physical therapy and so forth until I met the retirement board in early September of 1947. I was retired then as a Captain. After almost five years of service, I had received several awards and decorations, including the Purple Heart, the Air Medal with five Oak Leaf Clusters, the Prisoner of War Medal, The American Campaign Medal, The European Campaign Medal with seven Battle Stars and the World War II Victory Medal. I will admit that for a while, it was difficult to adjust to the fact that I was no longer an airman, but once again a civilian.

How do I remember Percy Jones? Very fondly. Those days were some of the most enjoyable of my life. There were so many friendships made that endure to this day and so many wonderful memories. We've had a couple of reunions, the most recent being in 1995, and it brought back more than forty former patients and spouses. All have very fond memories of Battle Creek and its residents.

Chapter 7

"A Very Active Life"

As I mentioned earlier, I had worked at the Kellogg's Factory before I entered service, and so I went back to work for them in the safety department. I married Barbara Van Syckle in 1947, and because I was still not getting around too well, I had some friends who told me about Jackson Community College. I wanted a small school where I could get around easier and they were very good to me there. They let me park my car wherever I wanted to. So I attended Jackson Community College, and I have nothing but the highest praise for that institution. Some of the professors there were as good as any I ever had. I later went from Jackson on to Albion College, and I graduated there Phi Beta Kappa. I continued to work at Kellogg's until I finally retired in 1983 as an executive of industrial relations after forty-some years of service. My first wife and I raised three children, and now have seven grandchildren. Unfortunately, she passed away in 1988. But in 1991, I married again to my present wife Phyllis, who I first dated in 1939.

Even with my disability, I feel like I have led a very active life. There were a lot of things I couldn't do as well as I would like to, and there were some that I had to substitute for. One was that I couldn't be a jock anymore. So I switched to being a volunteer, and I got involved in several wonderful organizations. The one I'm perhaps the proudest of is the food bank. Actually, people have called me the father of the food bank in Battle Creek. That's a really wonderful operation. It does so much good. I've also been active as a Kiwanian and today we are active as Charter Members of Chapel Hill United Methodist Church. All of these were such enjoyable and interesting things. I am also a certified member of MENSA, and I have been recognized as a distinguished alumnus of Lakeview High School, Jackson Community College, and Albion College.

Mr. Cutis paused.

"I guess that pretty much hits the highlights of my life after the military, Andy."

I asked him if there were any final comments he wanted to add as we rapped up the interview.

"Well, yes, there are a couple of things," he said.

One is that I'm glad I'm doing this interview because I think enough is finally being done to introduce the youth of today to the horrors of war. They need to know about the sacrifices that the servicemen made in defense of their country during World War II. There have been a number of wars since then, but I don't suppose they were quite the same. We at that time were truly defending our country on a level that has not been seen since. Youth need to understand what World War II really meant.

I suppose I could ramble on endlessly, but the other thing is that being a volunteer nowadays is a very popular sort of activity. Many of the presidents have endorsed volunteering and that's a great thing. From my standpoint, I think many of the veterans may well have led the way for this popularity in volunteer work. I often say to myself, "Jack, what would have happened had you not gone into the service? How would your life be different?" To be honest, I don't know. But I do know that because I was fortunate enough to make it home, I've tried –in all modesty- to use my God-given talent and intelligence to the best advantage of myself and others. Volunteering has played a big part in that, and I think most others from my generation would say the same thing.

Mr. Curtis's words made a deep impression on me as we rose from our seats and made our way out of the studio. We still chatted on our way back to the parking lot, but our conversation was much more serious now than it had been on the way in. "Thank you," I said, scarcely believing that this man I was addressing had actually lived through all the horrors he had described. "Thank you; not only for coming out today, but also for what you have sacrificed for us...for me, really."

I can't remember exactly what Mr. Curtis said in reply. What I do remember is the deep sense of respect I held for him as we shook hands and parted ways.

Part Two:

Larry Jenkins

Chapter 8

"The Adventure of a Lifetime"

For several reasons, 2003 was a milestone year in the history of the building we know today as the Hart-Dole-Inouye Federal Center. In addition to marking the centennial of the facility's original construction as the Battle Creek Sanitarium, 2003 also marked the sixtieth anniversary of the building's conversion to the Percy Jones Army Hospital. Because of this coincidence, two committees were established to organize several commemorative events within the community that would climax with a formal ceremony, held on May 31st, 2003. The first would focus on the Sanitarium's centennial and the other would be responsible for remembering the Percy Jones Army Hospital, as well as the people and events that made it famous.

A major initiative of the Percy Jones committee was to start an oral history archive by recording as many interviews with former patients and staff as possible. Mr. and Mrs. Larry Jenkins were among the first to volunteer for the program, and we were honored to bring them into the building on December 3, 2002.

After spending a few moments in Larry's old hospital ward, we made our way to a small break room that we figured would be an ideal location for our interview; secluded and quiet. This was the first time I had actually sat down to permanently record a veteran's story, and I was excited to get started with it. I remember thinking how fortunate I was to be doing my first interview with a guy like Mr. Jenkins.

We sat down around a long wooden conference table as Larry jokingly warned us that he had told his story a few times before and to be consistent with his average time, it may take him a few hours to get it all out. My dad chimed in, "That's okay; we go to bed at about nine o'clock, so we've got plenty of time." Larry laughed. "Good," he replied, "Then let's get started."

As soon as we finished setting up the microphones, Larry jumped right in and began sharing his account of the history he witnessed some sixty years prior. To aid his rich skill in storytelling, he had brought along "his book"; a three-ring binder stuffed to maximum capacity with photos, letters, articles, citations, and other memorabilia relating to his military career. Every so often, he would point out one of the photos or explain the significance behind an award. I didn't dare interrupt him; for fear that it would bring me out of that mode of fixation I had fallen into again.

He began very methodically, rattling off his birth date of January 29, 1924 and other important statistics as if they were programmed responses. Then he closed his eyes and seemed to dig back through his mind among memories that hadn't had the dust shaken off them in a long time.

"I remember very well the day that that the United States entered World War II", he said.

I was playing cards one Sunday night with a few of my buddies and here it came over the radio that Pearl Harbor had been attacked. It was kind of shocking, but there was also this feeling of excitement to it. We were all just in high school; sixteen, seventeen years old, and we didn't know what our nation being at war would mean for us. We saw it as the adventure of a lifetime.

I leaned forward in my chair, anxious to hear more.

I didn't think much more about it until I graduated from Lakeview High School in 1942. At that time anyone who graduated was either being drawn into the service of Uncle Sam's choosing or had the option of enlisting in a branch of his choice. Well, I joined the Air Force because I didn't think the infantry would be too exciting, being in the mud and carrying a gun. I figured that an airplane would be the safest place to be, so I joined on October 26, 1942 at Fort Custer in my hometown of Battle Creek. I was sent to Perrin Field, Texas for induction soon afterwards. There you had your calisthenics and basic training. Then I was sent back to Chanute Field to go through their sheet metal school where I became a sheet metal-smith, but I soon found out that that wasn't for me.

At that time, I had a chance to take the test to go into pilot training. The Air Corps was only selecting cadets with at least two years of college behind them, but I made it through without any college at all. There weren't a lot of us in that category. Most of the others had a couple of months at college and maybe two or three hours in a Piper Cub. So it's hard to describe why they picked me. I don't know for sure, but maybe it was the fact that I had a love for flying. I had built small model airplanes when I was just in grade school, and I knew quite a lot about them. Anyway, I passed the test to get into the aviation cadets and then I was sent to the classification center in Nashville, Tennessee. Here you had three weeks of psychological tests and other types of tests. If you passed all of them, you ended up in Montgomery, Alabama at Maxwell Field. That was kind of a pre-flight. You had two months of schooling, one month of which was very rigid and class-centered. You would stand at address all the time and the upperclassmen always had you doing foolish things. I really didn't like it. I wanted to quit then, but they encouraged me to stay. After I became an upperclassman, I never would follow their class system because again, I thought it was foolish.

From there I was sent to Carlston Field in Arcadia, Florida for Primary Flight Training. At Carlston Field, we had PT-17's which were open-cockpit bi-planes. They had 228 horse power engines. The Navy and Army both used them for training. After I had about eight hours, my instructor and I were shooting some touch-and go's on a farmer's grass field. We had made a couple and were going to take off again when he said, "Just a minute", and he stepped out. He said "You take it around... make three landings and then pick me up." Well that was probably the most exciting thing in my life at that time. Here you are, just nineteen years old and there's this bi-plane that's all yours. Flying was a great feeling. Probably one of the greatest. The fact that you could be airborne and have no one around you was just the greatest thing.

At twenty hours, the civilian instructors gave us a check. Those who couldn't make it were bypassed and went into some other category. They would become bombardiers or navigators. Then at forty hours, the military came in and a Captain came and flew with you. Some of those got washed out, too. My instructor started out with five students and it ended up that just two of us would actually make it through the program. It was that difficult.

After you had sixty-five hours in, you were sent to Basic Flight School where we flew the BT-13, and this was at Greenwood, Mississippi. I had an interesting experience there when I landed my plane at night in a pasture. You were required to fly so many nighttime hours while you were training, so I took off from Greenwood just before dusk. I turned on the lights of the plane when it was dark, but soon the battery was exhausted, and I had no lights. I couldn't see the instruments or flight plan maps. It was very dark that night, but I thought for sure I could spot the Mississippi River and find my way back. My tail wind was pushing me faster than I thought, though, and I found the wrong river which led me to Little Rock. After turning due east towards our checkpoint in Brinkley, Arkansas, I spotted the lights of their football field. The grass pasture I wanted to hit was just a short way from there. I knew that I had to come in high to miss the electric wires, so I used full flaps, landing just a short distance from the fence at the other end. I turned back the building, which was a teletype building, and went in to tell the lady all my problems. She walked over to the teletype machine and showed me the emergency warning just as my name came into view. It was known that I was out of fuel and all the area had been alerted to look for me. I borrowed a flashlight and went out to check my tanks. Both of them showed *zero*! Later on, an instructor arrived with another aircraft so I could complete my mission. With his aircraft, I completed my cross-country flight and arrived back in Greenwood at 2:30AM. It was probably good that I was young and fearless then!

After two months in Greenwood, you'd still get a check, though very few washed out then. From there, I was sent to Columbus, Mississippi, where they had twin-engine training, and we flew the AT-10. The base in Columbus is now one of the major Air Force bases in the country, but at that time they were just starting to build.

I graduated there on January 7, 1944 as a pilot and a Second Lieutenant. I almost didn't make it though, because back when I was in Primary Flight School, after I had sixty-two hours in, they told me to take a plane up and do what I wanted with it for three hours so I would have sixty five and could move on. Well, I guess I did too much with it, and I got court-martialed. I had been chasing people up and down the streets on bicycles and over the bridges. I just had more fun watching everybody run and jump out of the way. The flamingoes had their nests along the bay there, too, and I'd fly down there and pink feathers would go everywhere. When I got back to the base, the MP's were waiting for me because they could read the number on the plane real easy because I was that low. And sure enough, I was court maritaled for it. Of course sometimes that meant they'd wash you out of the flight training program, but they didn't wash me out. You see, the Major who was presiding over the case was from Kalamazoo, and we got to reminiscing a bit. He just told me that I would be confined to the base for a while, plus it would cost me a $100 fine. So when I got to basic flight training, the commander at the base called me into his office and he said, "I hear you were court martialed." I said "Yes," and he said, "Well, as far as I'm concerned it's not going to be on your record, you're not going to have to pay the hundred dollars and you will not have to be confined to the base." So that was all eliminated, and it never showed up on my records or anything. I was lucky.

After graduating from twin-engine school, I was sent to Salt Lake City, Utah. In Salt Lake City we got together with our crew; the pilot, co-pilot, and all your gunners and the engineer. I was put with a pilot that already had two months of training, so I ended up as a co-pilot with him. We went to Sioux City, Iowa and spent two months there flying B-17's. There you'd get a couple thousand-mile cross country flights and you'd get night flying. You'd get all kinds of training there in a B-17. The gunners would get to use their guns on a firing range, and we'd drop our bombs on a bombing range outside of Sioux City.

From there we went to Kearny Field, Nebraska, where we were going to pick up a plane. But at the time they were short on aircraft, so they sent us directly to Charleston, South Carolina. From there we took a boat with quite a few other crews to Africa because they needed replacement crews at that time real bad. They were being shot down at a very high rate. So we went over on a boat, and it was what they called a Liberty Ship. It took us a week or so to make the crossing.

Chapter 9

"Getting into the Show"

We arrived at Gibraltar, and they wouldn't let us go through because of the German subs, so we stayed one day and one night. Then they took us into Oran, Africa at night. We stayed in Oran a few days because at that time they were waiting for the Normandy D-Day invasion to take place on June 6th. So then they took us on an English ship up to Naples, Italy, and we were in the water when the invasion was going on. They got us into Naples, and we got off on a hospital ship that had been bombed and turned over. So we used the thing like a gangplank.

They had a train waiting for us that took us across Italy and into Foggia. This was to be our base, and it was where I joined the Second Bomb Group. I was put in the 96th Bomb Squadron as a replacement. I'll tell you: I was twenty years old, and I feared nothing at that time. So I was real anxious to get up and going because I wanted to "get in the show" –let's put it that way.

They always had a list of the pilots who would be flying the next day, and it was just a few short days until I looked and found my name on the list to fly the next morning. There were several targets scheduled, but the one next to my name was Ploesti, Romania. Of course I didn't know what that meant, but I soon found out it was where all the oil refineries were. The Germans were trying desperately to protect it.

We took off in formation the next morning and not too far from Sarajevo, which is in Yugoslavia, the Germans had ack-ack. It came up but didn't come very close. It was at least a quarter of a mile from us, but I was still scared, because it was the first time anyone had ever shot at me. We got over Ploesti, and I looked over there, and the city was completely covered with smoke. I don't know how they kept the smoke so low, but you couldn't see anything. It was as if you could cut it with a knife. It was just covered – everything. And then that first shell came up and "*Wham!*" -a piece went through our wing. I said, "Oh man, this is getting too close." We were going through these puffs of black smoke, and pieces of flack were going through our aircraft. Meanwhile, one of our gunners had gotten hit in the foot, and we weren't even over the target yet.

So we had our IP, which is the initial point of going into the target. That you can't deviate from. You can't try to dodge the flack when you're over it; you just got to go in. Then the bombardier takes over, and from that time, because you're on automatic pilot, he flies it until the bombs are gone.

We got just a short ways, and I saw this black cloud. I didn't know what it really was. But all hell broke loose when we got to it. The shells start bursting around you, popping all over the place, and the flack shrapnel would hit you. It felt like someone was out there with an ax just pounding on the side of the plane. And we managed to get through all this.

But these puffs, the instant they would break, you'd hit them – and that would be the shrapnel, of course. We dropped the bombs on a certain corner of that big smoke cloud. We turned off, and we'd just gotten off a short ways when the German ME-109 fighters came in. They were hitting us from the front. They figured that with the 20 millimeter guns they were using, they could actually dive through our formation and go right on down to the deck. They were very daring. At that time, we had some fighter protection, (I can't tell you what type of aircraft they were) but our fighters wouldn't go down that far because they knew that it would be hard for them to get back up afterwards. Later on, we would have P-38's and P-51's. We also had the Red Tailed P-51's a couple of times from the 99th Fighter Squadron. They were flown by the black from Tuskegee, and they were good pilots.

Well, we managed to get back and land and everybody jumped out of the plane and wanted to see where the flack holes were. I had been gung ho to get into things, but after that first mission, I was gung ho to stay. But I didn't dare admit I was afraid because I didn't want anyone to think I wasn't capable of my job. We just lived from day to day from there on out, hoping to survive the next mission.

We had a couple of good missions after that one, but then there was one where we took off for Budapest. Budapest was not an easy target either; you had a lot of flack there. We were carrying 2,000 pound bombs that day. When we went over Ploesti, we were carrying these fire bombs where you'd drop them out, and they'd swirl around, and these little fire bombs would go out. I don't know if they were magnesium or what, but we were supposed to come in with them after they had dropped the bombs to split the refineries open and then we'd set them on fire.

It was different over Budapest, though. We had 2,000 pounders that day, and as we turned off the target, the waist gunner called in and said that our left waist gunner, whose name was Fawls, had been hit by flack. 'Course I didn't go back there because we had gotten hit pretty bad and we needed both pilots to fly the plane, but a lot of the non-coms went over to take care of him. He had gotten shot in the flack suit and it ricocheted off and hit him in the neck, which killed him instantly, so it was too late. That was my first sad situation... he was only nineteen.

Larry paused in reflection.

When we got back to base we had to put up a red flare so they knew there was somebody on board that needed emergency help. We just pulled off the runway, and the ambulance was there and they picked him up.

Chapter 10

"Trouble"

Because we were new crew, we had been getting the old aircraft that were more troublesome airplanes. So we had several missions that were "turn backs" because of equipment failure. The manifold would usually break, and then you'd have no turbo or turbine, to get altitude. We had three or four of them that we had to turn back on.

One time we got this old plane on a mission to Brasov, Romania. It had the word *"Trouble"* written across the nose, by golly. Anyway, Brasov was north of Ploesti, about fifty to a hundred miles. About ten minutes before we got to the target, out went an engine. We had to feather it. Gas was spurting all over, and it was all we could do to keep it from catching fire. With only three engines and our full load of bombs, we lost a lot of speed and the rest of our group went on without us. Well, we weren't going to fly over a target at a low altitude all alone. So we turned around and watched the rest of our planes go right on past us. Because we couldn't take our bombs back to base, I came over the radio and said, "Instead of dropping our bombs in the Adriatic, let's pick out a secondary target.

We were shortly over the Danube River, and I looked along there, and here was a nice railroad track going from Ploesti on into Budapest. There were several houses near the railroad track and I said, "Let's take 'em out." With only three engines, we were low enough then, probably down to 19,000 feet, that the bombardier could do a good job at that altitude. So we took out the railroad. And when we did that, because we had to have such high manifold pressure and rpm's in the other three engines, the oil line broke in the second one and oil was spurting out all over the side of the plane. The oil pressure was going down pretty fast so I said, "We'd better feather that one in a hurry." And we did. So now we've got two engines. But you can't maintain two engines with all the weight. And we still had to try and get over a mountain, so we didn't dare lose any more altitude. The mountains there can get up to 8,000 feet, and here we are at 14,000, heading towards 12,000.

I got on the intercom to all the other members of our crew and I said, "Let's drop everything out of this plane...even if it weighs a pound, get it out!" So out went the bomb sight, the guns, the ammo; everything but our parachutes. We had to hang onto our 'chutes. So they scraped everything out. But we were still in enemy territory; 250, 300 hundred miles from home yet. So I said, "Take the doors off the aircraft." And away they went. Now I said, "If you have to bail out, fall just as far as you can before you open your 'chute; otherwise you might get shot in your 'chute," - which the Germans did.

At that time, we were still losing altitude. Even with all the weight we had out we were still losing.

So it came to my mind that maybe we could get the ball turret out some way. I said, "You've gotta try and get the ball turret out because there's about 1,500 pounds right there. I don't care how you get it out. Take something and whack it out, or throw it out. But get it out, or you won't be eating supper in Foggia tonight.

Well, they got it out in a hurry. I didn't know at the time how they could get it out, but that 1,500lbs was gone in no time. We were down now to 12,000 feet and just above stalling speed. 133 miles per hour is all we could keep with just the two engines. But that 1,500 pounds was gone, and we maintained our speed long enough to skim back over those mountains.

Even when we got back to the base we still had a problem, though. There was a 45 mph cross-wind to land on our metal runway they had put down in the middle of a hayfield. So we had to fight that all the way in. But we got down, and of course the plane wasn't worth very much then, because we had two engines that were no good, the other two were pretty hot, the ball turret had been dropped, and everything else had been lost out of it, right down to the doors. So they scrapped that one for parts.

Later on, I found out that someone had put me in to receive the Distinguished Flying Cross for this mission.

Chapter 11

"A Hand on My Shoulder"

The next mission, which happened to be my four-teenth combat sortie, was to Vienna, Austria. That day, July 16, 1944, they gave us a brand-new aircraft that was going to be ours for the rest of the war. On our way to Vienna, we followed our regular route that we had gotten down pretty good. We would go over this lake in Yugoslavia or Hungary; Lake Balastino I think it was called. I'd been to Vienna before; I'd made another trip and I knew it was going to be dog-goned bad.

On that first trip we had to make a 360-degree circle at the IP, because we couldn't see the target because of all the flack. We were just full of holes, but we did manage to drop our bombs and get back. But on this mission, with this brand-new aircraft, we stuck out like a sore thumb. The other planes were olive drab, and our plane was silver because it hadn't even been painted yet. Well, we hit the IP, and the radio man dropped this chaff that's like Christmas tree tinsel - boxes of it- to upset the radar. Then we dropped our bombs on an oil refinery pretty close to the center of Vienna on the Danube River. After our run, we turned and went right back over the city. I wish they would have had us turn to the right, but we turned right back over the city because we'd already been through all that flack and made it through. We figured that if we'd done it once, we could do it again.

Well, we got two direct hits right after that. One hit the nose and killed the bombardier instantly and wounded the navigator. Number three engine got hit too and it caught on fire. But I was hit too, and I was blinded. I could see bright things, like fire, but I couldn't see what was taking place inside the aircraft. I knew we were spinning out of control, through.

That day, having a new plane, things were a bit different, and I had thrown my 'chute under my seat. I usually put it behind the seat on the oxygen bottle, but we didn't have a hook there now because it was a new aircraft, and I had slid it under my seat instead. For some reason, I don't know for sure; I must have picked it up and put on my harness. 'Course I had to take my flack suit off too, and still I couldn't see yet. Like I said, I'm not sure how I got it on.

I stood up out of my seat, and both legs collapsed. Both my legs were broken by flack. I thought, "Well, I won't be able to get out of the front", because I knew we were hit there, too, and I thought I might get lost in the junk up there. I decided to go to the bomb bays because maybe someone would have opened them. With two broken legs, I fell down into the bomb bays and tried to push on them with my legs. But they wouldn't open. By then I had compound fractures in both legs from trying to walk on them, and I'd lost a lot of blood and oxygen too.

I laid there for a moment and I remember praying out loud. I said, "Lord, I'll be with you in a short while," and then I felt a hand on my shoulder.

Everyone had bailed out but this one guy, and his name was Ray Voss. He told me thirty-three years later when I talked to him by phone that when he got in there to the bomb bay, I was unconscious. He tried to lift me up, but he couldn't. So he went back and was going to jump out and leave me there, but he said "I just couldn't." So he came back, and I was awake then and had come out of unconsciousness. He tried to pick me up again, and I tried to help, but I didn't have the strength. I said, "Under that step there's an emergency release for the bomb bays... Pull it." So he did and the bomb bays opened and out I rolled.

I remember pulling the 'chute open, and I looked up and there was this white canopy above me. Then I couldn't see anymore because I passed out again.

Chapter 12

"For You the War is over."

I landed in the stubbles of a wheat field that looked like it had just been harvested. Evidently, someone had shot at me on the way down and they hit me in my left arm, but I didn't know it until I was on the ground. Luckily, I hadn't landed in a tree or anything because then I really would have been in trouble. The Lord was with me again.

Next thing I knew, I heard these strange voices around me. I'd never heard German before, but I knew what it was when I heard it. A bunch of soldiers gathered around me, and they were shouting at me even though I couldn't understand them. Then they grabbed me, took my 'chute off, and put it in the back of a truck. Then they threw me in like a sack of potatoes on top of the chute, which was just red with blood. Then the pain started to come because I was beginning to come out of the shock a little bit. This truck had these hard rubber tires and while it was bouncing around through this field of wheat stubble, I passed out again. I woke up in a little house, which was a place where the Germans could bring their wounded. It was kind of a first-aid station.

While I was still out, they had laid me up on a table and pulled the bones back into my legs. They'd also wrapped paper around them to stop the bleeding. It was about like crepe paper. Of course they gave their own wounded first priority, but the Luftwaffe doctors really did seem to want to help me, I guess because I was a flyer like them.

Well anyway, when I woke up there was this German standing above me who spoke a little English. And he said to me, "For you the war is over." I said "Yeah, I guess so," and he asked me if I wanted a drink of water. I said "No, no, no", because in my mind, I didn't know what they were actually going to give me. They could have easily poisoned me or something. It wasn't too long after that that I passed out again. This was about 10:30 on Sunday morning, and at approximately 6:00pm, they took me over to a hospital. I kept passing out this whole time because of the pain and loss of blood I suppose. But I do remember arriving at the hospital, and I saw that it was an old, old place built out of stone like they did way back when. They put me on a cot and left me there. When I woke up, I was looking into the eyes of a nun.

Her name was Sister Maria Abnoropolis. She spoke no English and I spoke no German, but I looked into her eyes and I knew she would be my friend. She was telling people around me to do some things, and they had four or five other Englishmen and Americans in that hospital on the top floor, so they brought one of them down. He spoke to me, and he knew a little German. He told me that they would try to help me, that they wouldn't hurt me, though they would have to interrogate me.

Now this was Sunday night, and they said that the interrogator would be over on Monday morning. Well, sure enough, on Monday morning, here he came. He was from the University of Vienna, and he spoke good English. He wanted to know a lot of things, but I just gave him my name, rank and serial number. He was satisfied with that, I guess, but he took my escape kit and all my stuff when he left, except for my jacket and the pants I had been shot in.

Now there were three or four nuns there at this hospital, and some of them were schoolteachers. They wouldn't teach the Nazi ways because they were catholic, so the Germans brought them in to work at their hospitals. When I was able to, Sister Maria brought my flying jacket up to me that had the hole in the sleeve from when I had been shot down. Our insignia for the 96th Bomb Squadron was a devil holding a bomb and thumbing its nose, and this was "nix" to a German nun. So she gave me a knife and pointed to where it was painted on my jacket and told me to cut it off. I took it off and cut it into little half-inch squares which made her happy, but then my leather jacket was no good. So I cut the rest of it into long strips and made a cover out of it for the little Bible that I always carried with me.

Chapter 13

"Vienna"

The nuns stayed with me day and night for pretty much a month. They kept a close watch on me because my legs were swelling up so bad, and one had turned just about as black as the ace of spades. I thought, "Well, there it goes," figuring they'd have to amputate it. There was no sense in putting me in a cast because they were so swollen, so they just had my legs sitting on metal trays most of the time. Crepe paper is what they used to bandage me because they didn't have anything else.

After a few weeks, my legs began to get their color back, and the flesh had started to heal. After four weeks, the swelling had gone down quite a bit, and that was good.

However, your food there was not good. They didn't have enough food to feed the people in the city, let alone keep you alive as a prisoner. But they brought me a dish of what they called "gamooza", and it looked about like the grass you see when a cow's been chewing on its cud. That's about what it tasted like, too. One of the nuns tried to get me to eat it, and it was horrible, but after a couple of days I got to where I could stand it. Then she'd give you a couple slices of bread or something, and once in a great while a Red Cross parcel would come in. Then you'd have a chocolate bar and maybe a couple of cookies.

They kept me there in this hospital, and after four weeks they decided to put me in a cast. The one leg was still on an angle and was pretty bad. Two of the nuns took me down stairs for a bath, (I hadn't had one yet) and they put me in this tub with the metal trays and paper around my legs. The paper disintegrated, and off went the trays. So here I was floating in this tub with my two legs dangling all over the place. I didn't dare say how bad I was hurting. There was just no use crying or complaining because it did no good. They did eventually get the trays back on, got me out of the tub, and took me back upstairs to the doctor. He was a good doctor, too. He decided to drive a pin through my heel and put weights on my leg to draw the bone out to where it should be, but that didn't work too well. The other leg they were able to put in a cast and set it. Neither one of them would mend, though, because we didn't have enough food to even grow calcium.

There was another doctor that came to the hospital and was going to drive another pin down through my leg to mend them. This doctor was one that helped create this method, the Kursher pin, as it was called, and they had already used the procedure on a lot of the German patients in there from the Russian front. He was just getting ready to do me, but we had another bombing which killed his wife and his fifteen-year old girl. He didn't come back for about a week, and by then I was scared because I didn't think he should be operating on anyone then. He was that shaken by it. I don't know what happened to him, if he got sent to the Russian front, or what, but he did not remain in Vienna for very long after that.

We would get these bombing raids quite frequently, and I mean, they were horrible. Being up on the top floor of this hospital, they couldn't move me to the basement during the bombings. Everyone else they could carry on stretcher. They'd take everybody out, and of course they'd lock the door and everybody was supposed to be downstairs. We had two guards and they went downstairs in the bombings too. But Sister Maria would come back upstairs and sit by my bed. I would shake so badly when the bombs were coming down. It was the most horrible sound, and it was just like all these bombs were centered to the pit of your stomach. It was just the most horrible thing you could ever hear. If the sun was out, it would turn to night during these raids because of the dust and smoke that would fly. I would get to shaking because I knew what the bombs could do. But Sister Maria, she wasn't a bit scared. She would say, "This is a hospital, they're not going to bomb it." But I knew better than that.

When these raids came, you could hear the bombers coming across in groups of six or seven, and you could maybe see a house go up about a block away. You'd get so you could tell when they were going to be misses just by the sound, too. We had an ack-ack gun real close to the hospital, and when that guy started shooting, that's when I knew we were really in trouble because that meant the bombers were getting close. I called him "Eager Joe" because it seemed like he'd start shooting every time we got bombed.

Sister Maria would always wonder why I was shaking, so she'd sneak a bottle of black beer up and give me a few tablespoons of it to try and quiet me down. Pretty soon, everything would settle outside and they'd start bringing in all the people who had been wounded or killed by the bombings. We'd have to listen to all these sirens going off from the ambulances then. They'd bring all the other patients back up, and of course I'd tell them what had been happening outside. But they already knew it had been bad. That they could see because of my shaking.

Chapter 14

"Stalag 17B"

We had a fellow in the hospital with us from Louisiana by the name of Nixon. He bribed the guards to get him out of Vienna and up to Stalag 17B where he would be safe from the bombings. He was like the rest of us; he didn't want to die by American bombs after he had already been through so much. So for about two weeks I begged them to move me to the prison camp too. Sister Maria didn't want me to go, but I said, "If I can get out of here, I'm going, because I've had it with these air raids." Well, they found that if they could get me out, then maybe I could be repatriated in September and taken back to America. But the bombings had kept the city pretty well shut down, so trains couldn't actually get out every day. There was a bus that was run on charcoal, (not gasoline) that would come by the hospital every day. So two of the other Americans dragged me out of that hospital on the 27th of October, 1944, and put me on this bus. Of course all these German people were looking at me and the other Americans, and they had to prop my casts up over the front seat which really turned their heads.

They got me to a tunnel that afternoon where they had an air raid shelter, and we stayed there 'til dark. They had a lot of POW's in there from Russia and other places. There was one train track going out of there to Krems, Austria, which is where Stalag 17B was. It was about 30-some kilometers from Vienna.

I got on this train at night, and it stopped many times along the way, either for repairs or for people, I guess. I suppose it was 11 or 12 o'clock at night when we got to Krems. There they put me on one of those things that they haul suitcases on and they let me lay in the dark there for a long time. All I had on was just a thin pair of German pajamas, and it was cold and beginning to snow, so I was getting wet. I sat there in the dark for the longest time, and I was freezing. I must have gotten frostbit or something, because I was shaking like a leaf. But that shaking was better than the shaking during the air raids in Vienna.

I don't think I've ever felt so alone in my life, because I knew no one in the town, and they were all Germans. I just kept thinking to myself, "Boy, is this scary." Finally, they came after me at about 4 o'clock in the morning with a truck and took me up quite a hill to a plateau where Stalag 17B was.

The main compound and the hospital were separated by about a quarter mile, and they put me in a single hospital room with a Romanian who was in real bad shape. He was really dying. This room was apparently where they'd put you if they didn't feel you were going to make it. But they told me that they would be moving me into another room after they made sure I didn't have any lice or anything. Because I was so cold and there was no heat, they gave me back my old flying suit too. I was thankful for that.

Then a little Frenchman came in who could speak some English. He said that the Gestapo would be in on Monday to take my flying suit back because they needed the zippers and snaps off it to make their own flight suits. He said "If I were you, I'd cut up the zippers." I said, "You bring me a knife and I'll cut 'em up." So he brought me a knife and I cut these little spots down the length of the suit, so it was no good to them. Of course that got me into trouble with the Gestapo, but I was pretty sick from being so wet and in the cold all the time so they didn't do anything to me.

When they got me moved into the other room, there were probably sixteen beds in there and they were about a foot apart. In this room we had all nationalities. There were six or seven Americans, there were Russians, there were Romanians, there was an Arab from Morocco, and there was an Italian that was blind. We all got together because we had come up with this international language, which was kind of like Latin with a lot of other words thrown in.

In the mornings, this blind Italian would come around, and he'd hit his cane on the bottom of my bed and say a couple of things in Italian, and I'd say several in English to him. The Russian that was in the bed across from me had been shot in the hip and he got gangrene and an infection. So they put plastic underneath of him and he never moved in all the time I was there in that camp, which was about six months. When I left, he was sitting in about a half inch of puss that had built up, and it ate the skin off his back. There wasn't much they could do for him because they didn't have any penicillin. They had nothing to fight infection; you just had to hope.

Anyway, I had plenty of time to do nothing in this place, because you just laid on your back looking at the ceiling all the time. I'd never slept on my back, so I'd twist my head and hold it with my arm and my arm would go to sleep. I'd usually end up feeling like I was paralyzed.

Now, it was cold in those barracks. You could blow your breath in the mornings and you could see your breath compressed into steam. There was a fireplace in one end of the building, and every day they'd give us each a little piece of coal to burn in it. The Frenchman had dug out a brick up in the chimney so that we could hide stuff in it. When the Gestapo would come in to check everything out, we'd have radio parts maybe, or parts to make a stove that had been smuggled in, and we'd keep them up there.

There were some other Frenchmen that would go out on work detail to some of the farms around there. They loved to work on the farms because they got to live with the ladies, they got better food and they got to steal things. So when they came in sick to the hospital, they might bring a handful of beans, or even an egg or some other article. One of the things they brought was this wire that we traded four or five cigarettes for. Someone brought a cord in and made a little stove out of it but not to use too often because electricity was sparse. You might be able to heat a little brew on it once and a while, but that was it. These are just some of the interesting things that went on in that barracks that winter – some of the good things, anyway.

Chapter 15

"So Dog-gone Young"

B ecause I laid in bed all the time with these casts on, I had to have a person take care of me. The Frenchman was supposed to do it, but he never did any of his work at all. If there was someone else he could get to do it, they might come in and help clean up a bit or help me with something. In the bed next to me was Ernie McCabe, and he was a co-pilot on a B-17 from Montana. Once and a while we'd get a Red Cross parcel and it would go to him and I, and maybe another person. We'd all have to share for a couple of weeks and there wasn't much in there so it didn't last long. The Germans couldn't get these parcels to us very regularly because of the bombings. In the main compound there were 85,000 prisoners, 4,000 being Americans who seemed to get first priority. Most of the other prisoners were Russians, but again, there were all nationalities mixed in there. The Russians were the ones that would go out and be forced into manual labor, fixing fences and railroad tracks mainly. The Americans didn't do any manual labor because they held more respect with the Germans.

As the war went on, I didn't notice the time passing so slowly because I'd been there so long and my stomach had shrunk so that I wasn't really hungry either. They'd bring in a loaf of black bread in the morning with a little of what they called jam once and a while. (I didn't know what it really was.) There was also this coffee which they figured was made with acorns. Very bitter. Very tasteless. They brought in a little cup of soup for lunch, maybe four or five tablespoons full. It had barley in it, but the chaff had never been taken off it, so we'd have to pick them out along with all the dirt and stuff that was in there along with it. Then for supper they'd have another slice of bread and a table spoon or two of what they called potato soup. The potatoes had never been cleaned, so it just looked like dirt. That's what we had, day in and day out.

On the 10th of January, we heard that there were some new Americans coming in. Sure enough, that afternoon, in walked a man on crutches. His name was William Chapin. When he came in we all just stared at him, because we wanted information. We wanted to know what things were like back home. They put him in a bed next me, and of course we jabbered all the time. Turns out we had a lot in common because he had been a pilot on a B-24. Bill was seven years older than me and a First Lieutenant, so he kind of oversaw the whole group of us. Plus he had a degree in journalism, so he did all the speaking for us in the compound as well.

Our news came up from the main compound of Americans. They had built a little crystal radio out of parts they had gotten from the French, and they'd get the news on that thing. BBC out of England had a potent radio system directed towards Germany, so it didn't take much to pick it up. They must have had a typewriter because they'd bring us up a little paper once a week. We'd have to get rid of it before the Gestapo came, but that was how we got our news.

Spring came and water was scarce at the Stalag. They'd have to bring it up from Krems, and the bombings made that very difficult. But they finally came in one day with some water for me to take a bath in. This was six months after my last bath. Well, it was ice water and I couldn't really wash my legs or anything because they were still in those casts. I was in a lot of pain, so I took a spoon and tore a hole in the cast and found out my legs were infected. All the doctors could do is just keep them clean after that. But I was young and I healed. The only reason I healed is that I was so dog-gone young.

My legs still hadn't knitted yet, and they had shrunk so bad that they said, "Well, maybe if we drill holes into the bone, we can make them grow more calcium." So they gave me a spinal, (it took four guys to hold me down), and they drilled these holes in my legs. But they still wouldn't heal even then. The Frenchman and this Polish guy who was supposed to be a surgeon decided that they had to get me out of bed because I had been flat on my back since July, and this was getting towards the end of March. But my knees had frozen, so they built stilts out of plaster, and put them up around my knee. I weighed just about ninety pounds, so I was nothing but skin and bones and they had to tighten the stilts up so they would fit. I traded for something to put on my feet, because we figured that if I could get up, then maybe I could walk. They used these big clippers to break my old casts off, but when we got rid of them, it didn't look like I had any skin or flesh at all on my legs at all, so that had to heal.

They stood me up one morning and I screamed. There were no calluses on my feet or anything; it was all just plain skin and it hurt. So they had to get me back down. They kept this up for probably a week until I was finally able to stand for any length of time at all. There was no pain then, but you could still feel the bones flopping around because they hadn't knitted. They brought me some crutches then, and I was able to crutch. I got to the door of our room, and got out into that fresh air and it was wonderful. You wouldn't believe the smell in our room from all those different kinds of infections. It was just so nice to have fresh air. Then I walked down a couple of steps to this cement railing and sat there and I got to where I could swing my legs over this railing. It took a while to break my knees free after they'd been frozen for so long, but I managed to do it after a while. As I sat there, I heard this noise, and three P-38's came down in the valley and they came up, and could just make it over our compound. All the guys were cheering and waving in the camp. There were two big tanks of fuel down at the bottom of the hill and those P-38's came down and set them on fire with their tracer bullets and they burned for two days straight. We were glad to see them do that.

Chapter 16

"Real Beds and Clean Sheets"

B y the middle of April, you could go out at night and see the big guns firing into Vienna from the Russian troops that were encircling the city. We knew they were coming for us, but we didn't know how long it would take them.

Well, one night there was a terrible battle, and the whole valley was lit up like day. It got scary because it looked like the tracers and shells were going to be coming into the camp. I went on my crutches with some of the others over to a basement in one of the other buildings and we got down in there. The Germans ended up pulling back, and the Russians came in. The next morning, May 10, 1945, we saw this truck come down the road. As it got up real close to camp we could see that it had a red star on the side, which meant it was Russian. They drove it right through the fence, and of course all of us prisoners just went wild because we had finally been liberated. Two ambulances came in, and they had stretchers for those that couldn't walk, and all this time everyone was just crying because we were so happy.

One of the Russian soldiers had a few loaves of bread and we just tore into that and ate all we could. I can still see us all sitting there crying and eating bread. It was white bread, too. Then they told us that we had to get going, and we all loaded up and left. We were gone in no time, and so happy to be out of the Stalag. We had to go though the Russian lines on our way back, and you could see little groups of ten or fifteen of them along the way. They'd stop you and want to search the truck every so often, and then they'd have us drink a toast of vodka with them. There was certainly a lot of celebration.

We stopped in a little town up in the mountains there. I don't know what it was called, but I got a couple items from some of the people there that they wanted me to have. One old man gave me a handmade pipe as a gift, and another wanted me to take his little girl up to the American lines where he thought it would be safer for her. I told him that I just couldn't do it. I felt bad, but there was just no way.

We had to cross this bridge, and on the other side of it was an American hospital. They put us in a room that had real beds and clean sheets, and it was wonderful. This was the first time after being released that I really felt free... I felt free. There were the beds, there were nurses, and there was real food. They told me I could have anything I wanted and I said, "I'll have a hamburger and a glass of milk." I'm not sure what the others asked for but it was probably the same thing. Well, they got me my hamburger and I took a couple of bites of it along with the milk, and I couldn't keep it down. I threw it all up. I just couldn't eat! But they kept us at this hospital for a while, and they deloused us and bathed us all for the first time since we had been captured. They tried to see what they could do for my legs, but they couldn't do much.

Bill Chapin and I got out one day with this other guy from Pennsylvania, but a nurse had to go with us. We walked down by the Danube River, which we weren't but a block from, and she took pictures of us. Well, that night Chapin and I decided we wanted to get out and see a little more. So we crutched our way down without the doctors or anybody knowing it, and went for a walk out in the city. I got down a ways and saw some Polish people that had taken over a house. Of course they were excited to see an American and they invited me in. We sat there and jabbered away in our own languages for a long time. They were so excited, and I was so excited that we forgot about the time; it got dark and I had to leave. So I crutched my way back, and went up one street. It didn't occur to me how dangerous all this was at the time. But anyway, I came back to the hospital and I saw Bill sitting on the steps with a couple of young children, and I said "You better come on, Bill, we gotta get home." So we turned and started walking, but it wasn't too long until the MP's came and picked us up in a jeep. That turned out to be the only time we ever got outside of the hospital. They quarantined us after that, you see.

They took us out of there to a field hospital, which was still basically on the front lines. It was a tent and they had us all in there on stretchers. One of the other fellows in there had a gun and he asked me if I wanted it. He said, "A German killed two of my buddies and shot me with it, so I don't want anything to do with the thing." I said "Yeah, I'll take it." And that's how I got this German .32 caliber pistol which today is on display at the Air Zoo in Kalamazoo, Michigan.

From there, they drove us by ambulance to Munich. While I was there, I was so cold, shivering and shaking that an American doctor had gone in and found a couple of German flying jackets that he gave to me, and they were warm. He said I could have them. The next day, a C-47 "Gooney Bird" flew in and took us to Reims, France. We got off there at an American hospital, and there they would feed us about five or six times a day, and you could have anything you wanted in small amounts. Well, all the other wounded guys were envious of us POW's because we were being fed so well.

It was at this hospital that I walked to the end of the room on my crutches to see my friend Smitty, who was the polish guy from Pennsylvania. I talked with him for a while and then I walked back through the ward. I got up in the morning and was going to go see Smitty again when somebody spoke to me. I didn't recognize him and he hadn't recognized me until then, but we had grown up and gone to Lakeview High School together.

That voice was the voice of Jack Curtis.

What had happened is Smitty had gotten up in the night to smoke a cigarette, and Jack was smoking too. They got to talking, and Smitty asked him where he was from. Jack said, "Well, I'm from Battle Creek, Michigan." And Smitty said, "Hey, I've got a buddy in here from Battle Creek, too." So the next morning when I came through, Jack spoke to me. When I heard his voice, I knew him. Voice you can always know. And he knew me. We said to the doctors, "We went to the same high school and knew each other when we were kids, so we want to stick together." So they did keep us together and we both flew into Number 1 Hospital in Paris where we stayed for a few weeks. One night I went out on the streets of Paris to get Jack and me a Coke. I wasn't supposed to be out, and I shouldn't have gone, because I got lost. Some Frenchman who didn't speak English evidently saw that I was an American and thankfully, he got me back to where I came from. Never did get the Cokes, though.

For some reason, Jack and I got on different planes coming back to the States. There was some sort of emergency or something, so we couldn't go together. They flew me into Mitchell Field, New York by way of the Azores, and he stopped off at Crest Isle. At Mitchell Field, we got in there in the middle of the night. I'd been in a stretcher the whole time we were flying, and they took me off with a forklift. I spoke to the guy, but he was mean and he didn't respond. Nobody spoke to me at all, as a matter of fact. But they took me into a room with the other POW's and then they locked the door. They locked us in and we couldn't get out! I don't know why, but I got kind of irked at the situation. I thought to myself, "These are Americans; why aren't they treating us a little more human?" But then they gave me a dime to call home and I talked to my mother then. It was the first time I had spoken with her since probably January of 1944 and I cried.

Chapter 17

"Percy Jones"

I n a few days, I told them I wanted to go to Battle Creek. I didn't know Percy Jones was there then, but they told me that's where the Orthopedic Hospital was, and they'd be sending both me and Jack there. So that's where we went. They flew me into Battle Creek on a C-47, and we went right over my home. We landed at Kellogg field, and they picked me up and drove me downtown in an ambulance. It was a real relief, I would say, to be home. Right away, I was put on the 10th floor in officer's ward. We had a bunch of nuts up there, including me. The guys were all just back from overseas you know, and they were just wild. I called my mother and my dad again, and they came to see me. I was sitting on a bench right in front of the elevator, and when they came off, I started to cry. Tears came to my eyes and I started to cry again, I was so happy. I was just so happy to be alive and to be home.

After some time, they told me they were going to have to do a bone graft. It was because my legs hadn't healed yet; especially the right one. You could still push the bones around inside there. They said, "We're going to do a bone graft, but you're going to have to take a spinal." I started yelling at them, and I said, "Whatever you do, don't give me a spinal, because I had that one in the POW camp and it took four people to hold me down for it. I thought I was going to die the way the pain shot through my body, and I don't want that again." Well, they said, "We can't operate on you without a spinal. You gotta have one, and it's got to be a continuous spinal because it's going to take a long time." So I had to give in to them. Here, a spinal is just like pushing your thumb on your arm; there's nothing to it. But it had taken four guys to hold me down over there. Well, turns out they weren't real doctors, and they had done it wrong.

They had to give us Penicillin too, and in those days you had to take it every three hours. So I had to get one of these shots every three hours for about six months. The nurses would come in at night and stick me in the rump with that needle, and I'd say, "ugh" in my sleep. It got so I just told them to use the same hole all the time so it wouldn't wake me up, and they did! I got so I wouldn't even wake up when they gave me those shots.

I spent two years at Percy Jones all together. They gave me bone grafts and removed a lot of metal fragments. I had osteomylitis (inflammation of the bone marrow) in my right leg that took a long time to heal. I'd have my operations in town at the main hospital sections and then I'd be sent out to the Annex at Fort Custer for recuperation. They always kept people on leave because they figured there were about 10,000 patients there at Percy Jones, and they would rotate leave so there were only so many at the hospital and so many at the Annex at one time. Every sixty days I'd get a leave, and the doctors would just expect me back at a certain time. But since I was from Battle Creek, I would often stay at home with my folks instead of going out to the fort. They lived on Beadle Lake Road at the time, which was just seven miles from the hospital.

At Percy Jones we were all in one boat. We were not all prisoners, but we had all been shot up in either Germany or Japan, or other parts of the world. And we came from all over, too. One of the people I knew was Danny Inouye, a future Senator from Hawaii. Danny was a very close friend. He was out at the annex a lot of the time. I don't know how to tell this...but we would drink all night and sleep all day. Drink all day and sleep all night. You don't know what we did out there to those doctors. We had an officer's club there, and the first night they said, "We're going to initiate you, Larry." So they had me chug two bottles of this stuff, you know, and then they put a pillowcase over my head and rolled me down the hallway back to my room. They rolled me in there and I was just sick as a dog. I couldn't take it. Those guys could take it, but I couldn't. I didn't even want to. Danny was there too. He and Jack and I did do a lot of going out together after that, and I remember it all very well. The three of us were very close.

They had two officers' barracks at the annex and that's where I stayed. I had a bed in one of them all the time, but I didn't always sleep there because like I said, I would go home to sleep quite often. I can remember a group of us; Jack and me and a few others, would come in to our barracks, hungry, at about 4:00 in the morning. We'd get the nurses and we'd say, "We gotta have our beansy-weansies right now!" We'd go to the kitchen then, and we'd have them practically crying, those nurses.

Larry laughed.
"That was so long ago"

But you know, when I was in bed, my folks would come up to see me several times a week. When I had an operation, they didn't come up, because whenever I have an operation I don't like to see anybody. It's just that I'm on medication and I can't talk right with the pain. One time, though, they didn't come for three weeks. Finally, here they came and my dad had brought booze for all the fellas. We had these white sacks on the back of our wheelchairs that we kept our stuff in, and we all put our bottles in these things to hide them from the doctors. Well, one of the guys from Holland, Michigan, reached back to pull out a bottle and it slipped out of his hand and went all over. The nurse came in screaming, and she went and got Gillfallen, the doctor. They said that this kind of behavior had to stop, but of course it didn't. They were very patient with us. We'd gone through a lot, and they just said "Well, this is your time."

I guess it was just a utopia at Percy Jones. Like I said, I could go home to see my folks all the time, sleep at home and go back and forth from there to the hospital whenever I wanted. I had a Plymouth coupe I had bought and they let me drive it, too. You know, you had a gearshift in the center, and I cut a broomstick off that I used for the brake. I'd just throw it into gear and push the brake with the stick, and that's the way I drove. I was driving ridiculously, but of course there wasn't as many cars on the road then to worry about and I drove all over the place with that thing.

Of course there was the Percy Jones song, too. The first two lines were, "Percy Jones, Percy Jones, where they cut off all your bones... They give you

pegs instead of legs and then they send you home..."
There are several more verses to it, but I can't seem
to recall them just now. Funny I can't remember any
more because we used to sing it all the time.

When I got out of the hospital, I went to Jackson
Junior College, because I couldn't walk very far. I
needed special shoes to get around. Jack couldn't walk
well either, so we both went there because they gave
us good parking. When I finished there, I was going
to go on to Albion College with Jack, too, but I still
wasn't feeling good and I ended up at the VA hospital
in Dearborn where I lived for three months in 1949,
receiving care for post traumatic stress. I moved to a
veteran's center at the University of Michigan after
that where I stayed for another eight months of treatment. It was... kind of a terrible situation.

I had met my wife Peg at a local dance in 1946,
and we went together for three years before we were
married in 1949. We raised three fine children, losing
our Down's syndrome daughter, Connie, at the age
of 37. Our two sons, Roger and Larry, Jr. still live in
the area. As a matter of fact, Roger now lives right
next door to us here in Climax.

Chapter 18

"No Regrets"

I eventually came out of the hospital and enrolled in a vocational program in electronics at Western Michigan University. I figured it would help me find something I could do at home, so then if I had to go back into the hospital, it wouldn't matter. I could work as I pleased that way. Finally, I did get better, and I went to work for RCA in their communications end. It was great because I could live at home and work away as I please. And working away, I could come home during the day even if I didn't feel good. They were very happy to have me, and I was very happy to be with them, because I felt like I was very good at what they wanted me to do. I'm not bragging here–that's just what all the people said. So I got through there, and retired in 1982.

When I retired, I took up a few odd hobbies. I love to paint pictures, so I took up painting and did a lot of it. I still love building model aircraft and I've done quite a bit with radio controlled flying over the years as well. We lived on a lake in Florida for a few years and I built a lot of my house by myself. We used to go down there to Lady Lake for about three months out of the year because I could get around pretty well there. But even that has gotten to be too big of a chore for us and now we just stay put here at our home in Climax, Michigan. I do go to the VA quite often in Battle Creek for various doctor's appointments, and it seems like everyone knows me out there now. They have a group therapy program that has really helped a lot of people, including myself. I just can't say enough about the VA and all that they do for our veterans, even those that are coming back from the war today. The whole organization has just come so far since I started out with them in 1946, and it's great to see. Whenever I'm out there, even I always want to stop and thank a veteran for what they have done for America. Even if they didn't get out of the States, they spent time in the service and did their part. That's why it has improved so much out there; because people have remembered the value in things like service to our country. It just makes me so proud to see it, and it should make all of us proud too. Personally, I'm very happy to just enjoy life these days. I'm thankful to be doing what I am even though I don't feel too good on occasion. I would say that given the chance, I would do it all over again if I had to, even knowing how things would turn out. It's one of those things where looking back, one way or another, it's fact, and it all becomes a part of who you are in the end.

Mr. Jenkins paused a final time, his eyes showing a near hesitation to bring the interview to a close.

"I have no regrets," he said, "And I wouldn't trade these memories for anything."

Epilogue

My dad and I were both deeply moved by Mr. Jenkins's words. We agreed that what we had experienced that afternoon with Mr. and Mr. Jenkins would be something to remember for the rest of our lives. Walking the halls with them and seeing the very places were so many of those stories had taken place had been an incredible thing to participate in, and I just felt lucky to have had the opportunity to be there.

Though it would be another six months before the interview with Mr. Curtis would take place, it too would have a similar impact on me. I was not only impressed with the stories both men had to tell, but with the way they had taken their experiences, as traumatic as they were, and made the best of them; for themselves and for perhaps most of all, for others.

While this in itself can be a valuable lesson, there is still another truth that can be learned from Jack and Larry. It is the fact that there are thousands of veterans like them who also deserve to have books written about them; thousands of unsung heroes everywhere who have uncommon stories to tell if we are only willing to listen. Remember this the next time you see a man at the grocery store wearing a Purple Heart hat or a lady at the bank with a Navy pin on her jacket.

If you take the time to ask veterans like these about their time in uniform, listen to their response, and I can guarantee you won't be sorry. Not only will this simple act let him or her know that their service is appreciated, but it will also enrich your own life by providing a unique connection to the past that no book can capture. Maybe, in some small way, you can even give a little of something back to someone who has given so much for you by letting them know that their sacrifices will not be forgotten. In short; talking with a veteran about their service is potentially one of the most meaningful things you can do.

For me, it is still incredible to think that two kids who went to school together and played on the sanitarium lawn in Battle Creek could share so much in common during their wartime service without even realizing it. Then to be reunited in that French hospital and be sent back to their hometown, to the very spot where they had played as kids and maintain a close friendship that endures to this day is truly amazing.

Of all this you might ask, "What are the chances?"

I say it wasn't chance at all. Like the Israelites of the Old Testament, the Thing responsible for this story was far more powerful than mere chance.

It was *Eagles' Wings*.

Captain Lawrence L. Jenkins, circa 1945.
(Jenkins Collection)

**Larry calls this a picture of "his first plane ride."
That's his sister standing next to him.
(Jenkins Collection)**

**Larry's school picture, circa 1939.
(Jenkins Collection)**

**Here's a shot of Larry taken in Greenwood, Mississippi
during the fall of 1943. He's training in a BT-13 aircraft.
(Jenkins Collection)**

**A B-17 in combat over Europe. Larry logged fourteen
sorties in a plane not unlike this one.
(Jenkins Collection)**

**This picture, taken in May, 1945, shows Larry (left)
a few days after he was liberated from Stalag 17B.
With him is an American nurse and his friend Smitty.
(Jenkins Collection)**

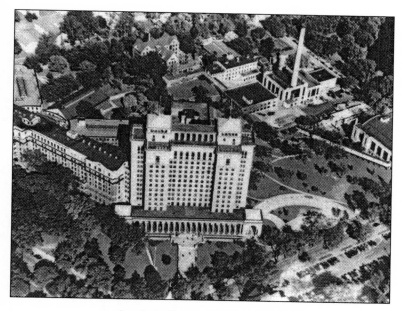

**Aerial photograph of the
Percy Jones Army Hospital complex, circa 1946.
(Courtesy Hart-Dole-Inouye Federal Center)**

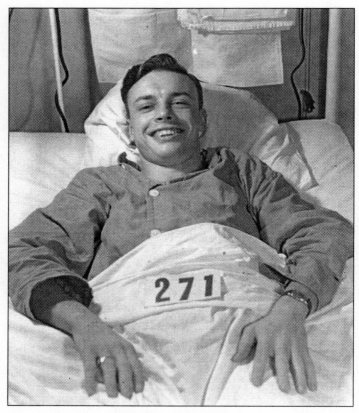

**Larry as a patient at Percy Jones in 1945.
(Jenkins Collection)**

**The Jenkins family. From left: Peg, Connie, Larry,
Larry, Jr., and Roger. (Jenkins Collection)**

**Jack's High School Graduation photo, 1941.
(Curtis Collection)**

Aviation cadet Jack C. Curtis, 1943. (Curtis Collection)

Taken in Boise, Idaho, this photo shows the crew with which Jack would serve overseas. Curtis is in the back row, third from left. (Curtis Collection)

**Jack in his flying gear, 1943.
(Curtis Collection)**

Curtis flew thirty-one missions over Europe in a B-24 bomber similar to this one. (Curtis Collection)

Convalescing at Percy Jones was a fun process according to Curtis, who is looking over his shoulder in the foreground. The smiling amputee to his left is future Senator Daniel Inouye of Hawaii. (Curtis Collection)

The officer's dining room at Percy Jones. Mere photography could not begin to capture the building's splendor. (Courtesy US Army Signal Corps)

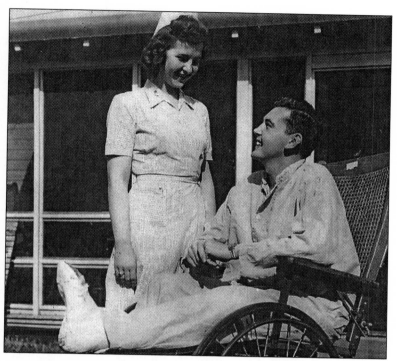

**"The Annex: now that was where all the fun was."
Jack visits with one of the cadet nurses at the
Percy Jones Annex, 1946. (Curtis Collection)**

**Jack and Larry fished together on their annual trip to
Canada for more than forty consecutive years. Here
they are with the day's catch in 1960.
(Jenkins Collection)**

Jack shares a laugh with Bob Dole during the Senator's 1996 campaign for president. (Curtis Collection)

**Larry Jenkins and Jack Curtis, January 2007.
(Photo by Peg Jenkins)**

Glossary

Ack-Ack: Slang for anti-aircraft gunfire.

Air Medal: America's seventh-highest award for combat valor and the second highest of those reserved only for airmen. At the peak of the air war over Europe, the medal was commonly awarded to airmen displaying feats of heroism and occasionally upon the completion of five or ten combat missions.

Azores: Islands in the North Atlantic, 900 miles west of mainland Portugal.

B-17 "Flying Fortress": A US Army Air Force high-altitude bomber, produced by the Boeing Company and capable of delivering up to 6,000lbs of ordinance. It was powered by four 1,200 horse-power engines and could reach a maximum speed of 287mph and a maximum altitude of 35,000 ft.

B-24 "Liberator": A US Army Air Force long-range bomber originally produced by the Consolidated Vultee Aircraft Corporation and later by the Douglas, Ford, and North American Aviation companies. The B-24's four 1,200 hp Pratt & Whitney engines could support an ordinance load of up to 8,000lbs. The aircraft's maximum speed was clocked at 290 mph with a maximum altitude of 28,000ft.

BBC: British Broadcasting Corporation.

Distinguished Flying Cross: America's fourth-ranking award for valor and the highest of those specifically reserved for aviators. The medal is awarded to airmen who display outstanding heroism or meritorious service while participating in aerial flight.

Fort Custer: A US Army induction and training center located in Battle Creek, Michigan.

Gestapo: German Military Police.

IP (Initial Point): Specified bomb target for a particular mission.

Luftwaffe: The German Air Force.

Stalag: A German prisoner of war camp.

MP's: Slang for US Army Military Police.

POW: Prisoner of War

Purple Heart: America's oldest and perhaps most legendary award available to members of its armed forces. As the sixth-ranking decoration for combat service, the Purple Heart is awarded only to those servicemen and women who are honorably wounded or killed during an armed conflict.

Wehrmacht: The German Army.

Sources

Curtis, Jack C. "How Do I Remember Percy Jones?" <u>Scene Magazine</u> 28 (2003): 20-7.

Curtis, Jack C. and Andrew Layton. <u>A Veteran's Reflections: Veterans History Project Interview</u> Recorded at the Battle Creek VA Medical Center, 5 Jun. 2003. (Transcribed by Sharon E. Bradley. CER 5008 Certified Court Recorder.)

Chapin, William. <u>The Milk Run</u>. Sausalito, CA: Windgate, 1992.

Gunston, Bill. <u>The Illustrated Directory of Fighting Aircraft of World War II</u>. London: Salamander, 1988.

Jenkins, Lawrence L., Andrew Layton, and Joseph Layton. <u>Percy Jones 60th Anniversary Oral History Interview: Capt. Larry Jenkins</u>. Recorded at the Battle Creek Federal Center, 3 Dec. 2002

Jenkins, Lawrence L. <u>Kalamazoo Air Zoo Oral History Project: Lawrence L. Jenkins</u>. (VHS) Recorded at the Kalamazoo Air Zoo, 23 Oct. 2000.

Lawrence, Amber and David Walton. <u>Born to Serve: The Jack Curtis Story</u>. (VHS) "Stories of Service" Video, 2003.

Layton, Andrew and Zach Talmage. <u>Above and Beyond: The World War II Experiences of Captain Larry Jenkins</u>. (VHS) "Stories of Service" Video, 2004.

<u>I'll Invest My Money in People: A Biographical Sketch of the Founder of the Kellogg Company and the W. K. Kellogg Foundation</u>. Battle Creek: W. K. Kellogg Foundation, 1990.

About the Author

Andrew Layton is a home school graduate who has enjoyed a passion for history for as long as he can remember. Raised in an Air Force family, Layton published his first book, *Wolverines in the Sky: Michigan's Fighter Aces of WWI, WWII and Korea* at the age of sixteen. Today, Andrew serves as a volunteer at the Battle Creek VA Medical Center where he visits veteran patients on a regular basis. He has also been active with the Library of Congress' Veterans History Project for which the original interviews that inspired this book were conducted. Layton is the recipient of several honors and awards including the VA's James H. Parke Youth Volunteer of the Year Award, the DAV's Jesse Brown Memorial Youth Scholarship and Michigan's Legion of Merit Medal.

Printed in the United States
200055BV00002B/13-225/A

9 781602 663909